Science During the Renaissance

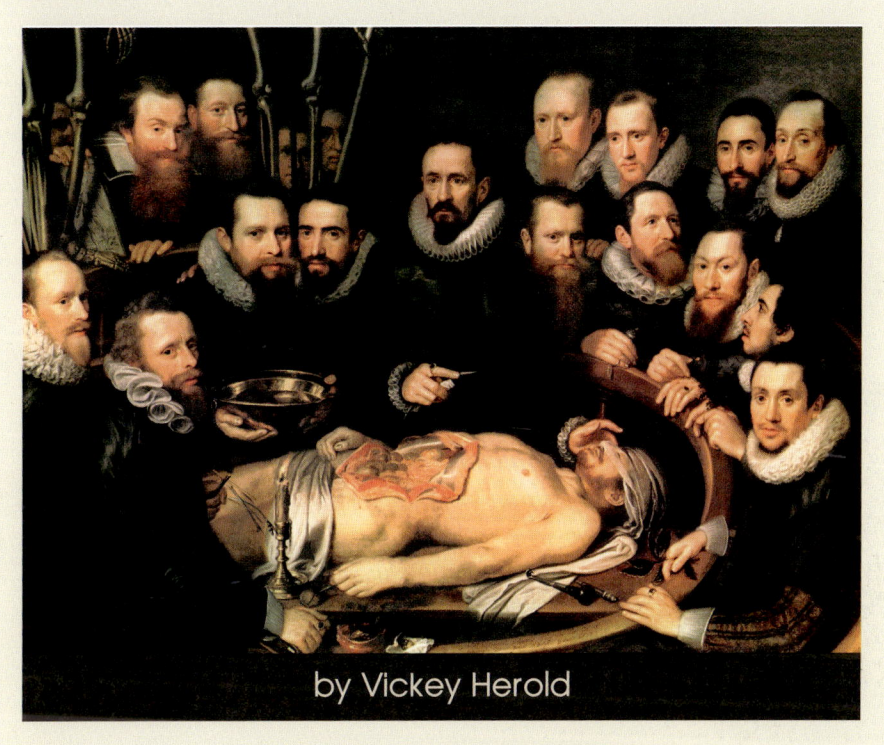

by Vickey Herold

Table of Contents

Introduction	2
Chapter 1 How Did Science Change During the Renaissance?	4
Chapter 2 What Did People Discover During the Renaissance?	10
Chapter 3 What Did People Invent During the Renaissance?	20
Summary	28
Glossary	30
Index	32

Introduction

The Renaissance was a time in history. **Science** changed because of the Renaissance. People studied science in new ways. People discovered new things.

▲ The Renaissance was a time in history.

What was science like during the Renaissance? Read this book to learn.

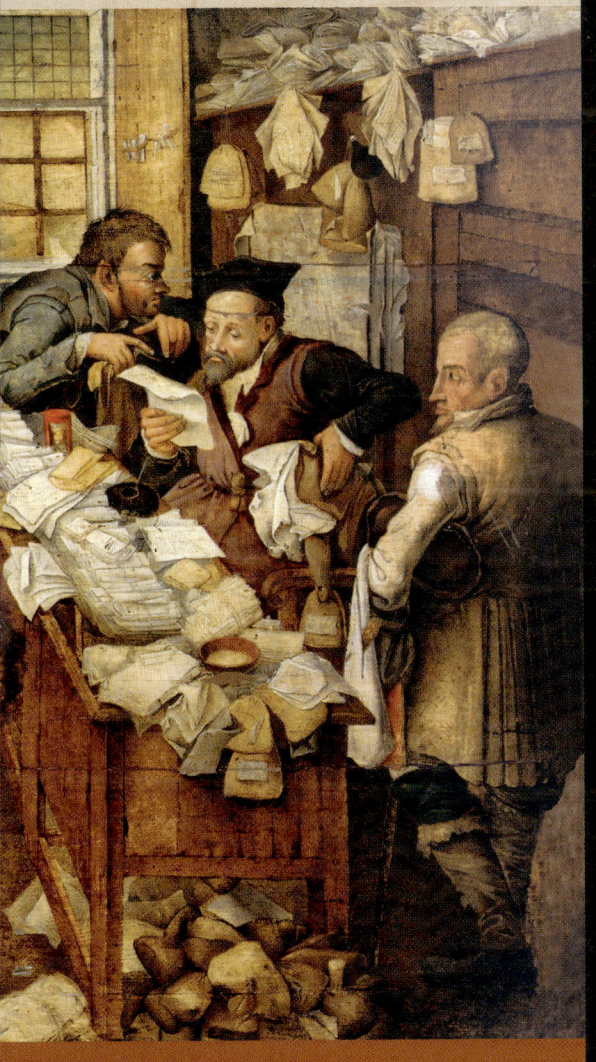

Words to Know

accurate

anatomy

astronomer

inventions

prove

the Renaissance

scholars

science

scientific method

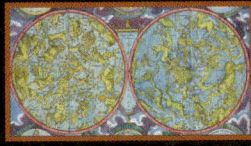

universe

See the Glossary on page 30.

Chapter 1

How Did Science Change During the Renaissance?

The Renaissance was a time in history. The Renaissance was a time of learning. The Renaissance began about 1400 A.D. It ended about 1700 A.D. Science changed because of the Renaissance.

▲ Science changed during the Renaissance.

Did You Know?

Renaissance means rebirth. People had a rebirth of learning. People began to learn new things during the Renaissance.

Science began to change. The year was about 1600 A.D. **Scholars** studied the world in new ways. Scholars studied the **universe** in new ways.

▲ Scholars studied the universe.

It's a Fact
People say the Renaissance caused a scientific revolution. The scientific revolution changed science. The scientific revolution changed how scholars studied science. The scientific revolution was very important.

Chapter 1

Science was different before the Renaissance. Scholars did not look for facts. Scholars did not have to **prove** new ideas.

◂ Scholars did not use facts before the Renaissance.

Science changed during the Renaissance. Scholars had to look for facts. The facts had to be **accurate**.

◂ Scholars began to use facts during the Renaissance.

6

How Did Science Change During the Renaissance?

Scholars worked in new ways. Scholars used observation. Scholars used what they saw. They began to use math. They began to use new tools.

▲ Scholars began to use new tools.

Make a Connection

Look at the tools scholars used. What tools do you use in science? What tools do you use in math?

Chapter 1

Scholars used facts. Scholars used facts to prove new ideas. Science became more accurate.

How Did Science Change During the Renaissance?

The new way to study science was very important. The new way was the **scientific method**. The scientific method uses facts to prove ideas. The scientific method changed science forever.

It's a Fact
Scientists still use the scientific method today.

◀ Scholars had to prove ideas about science.

Chapter 2

What Did People Discover During the Renaissance?

Scholars discovered many important things during the Renaissance. Scholars discovered facts about Earth. Scholars discovered facts about the universe.

▲ Scholars learned facts about the universe.

Scholars discovered facts about the human body. Scholars discovered facts about **anatomy**.

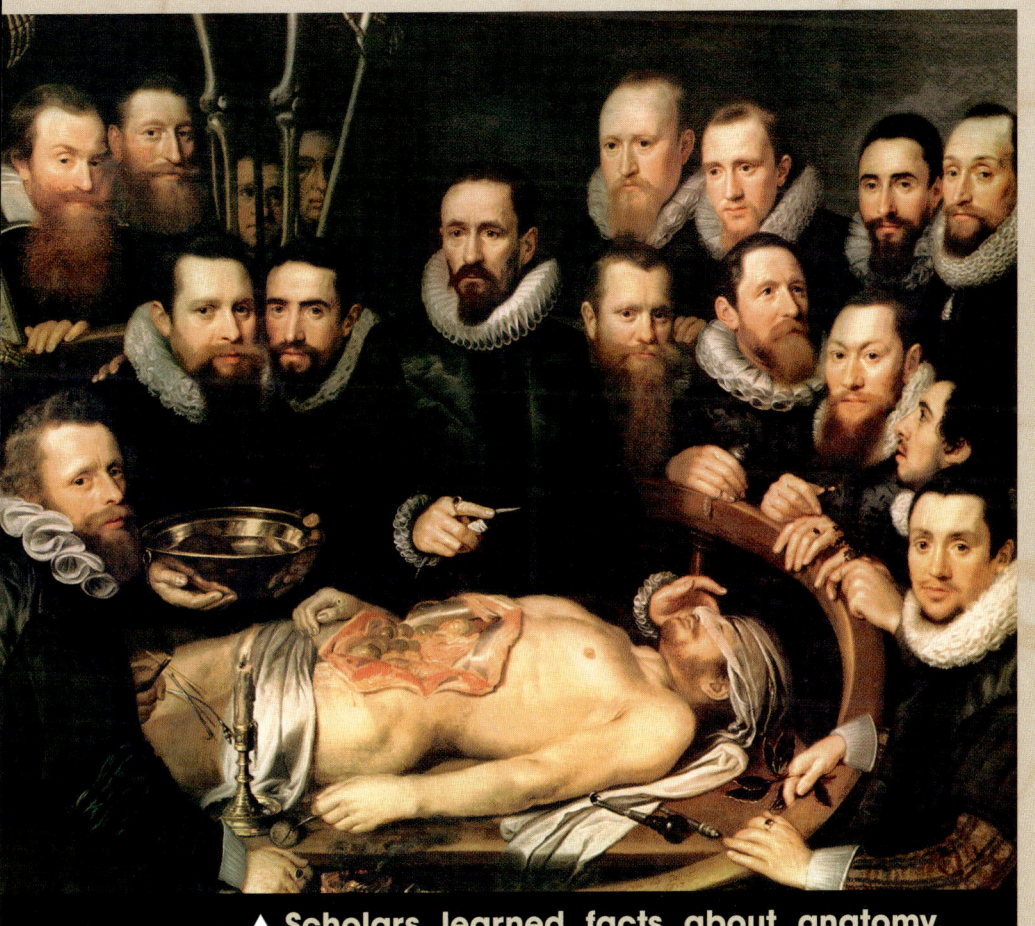

▲ Scholars learned facts about anatomy.

Chapter 2

People believed different ideas before the Renaissance. People believed Earth was the center of the universe. People believed the other planets moved around Earth.

◀ This map shows what people believed about Earth.

Nicolaus Copernicus was an **astronomer**. Copernicus had new ideas about the universe. Copernicus had new ideas about Earth.

◀ Copernicus was an important astronomer.

What Did People Discover During the Renaissance?

Copernicus said the old ideas were not accurate. Copernicus said the sun was the center of the universe. Copernicus said Earth moved around the sun. He said other planets moved around the sun, too. Many people did not believe Copernicus.

▲ Copernicus believed the sun was the center of the universe.

Chapter 2

Galileo was also an astronomer during the Renaissance. Galileo lived after Copernicus. Galileo found facts to prove what Copernicus said. Galileo proved Earth moves around the sun.

◀ Galileo

▲ Earth moves around the sun.

What Did People Discover During the Renaissance?

Johannes Kepler was another astronomer during the Renaissance. Kepler discovered how planets move around the sun.

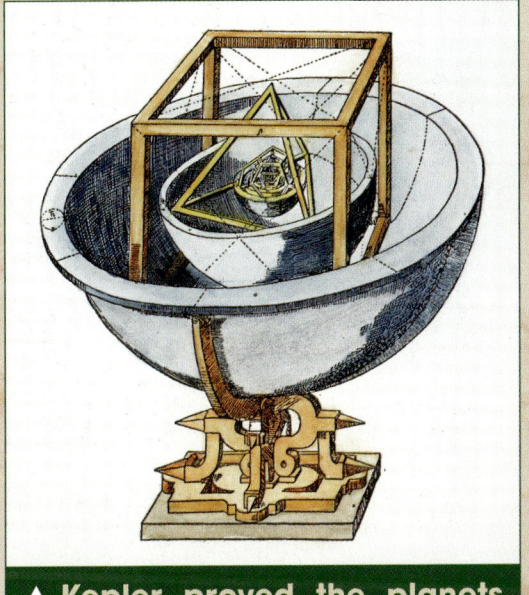

▲ Kepler proved the planets move around the sun.

▲ Johannes Kepler

Solve This

Look at the time line. Which man lived the longest? How old was the man when he died?

Astronomers in the Renaissance

1473	1543	1564	1571	1630	1642
birth of Copernicus	Copernicus died.	birth of Galileo	birth of Kepler	Kepler died.	Galileo died.

Answer: Galileo — 78 years old

Chapter 2

Leonardo da Vinci was a great artist. Da Vinci made many great paintings during the Renaissance. Da Vinci made many great sculptures.

▲ Leonardo da Vinci was an artist.

▲ Da Vinci made great paintings.

Da Vinci made great sculptures. ▶

What Did People Discover During the Renaissance?

Da Vinci was also a great scholar. Da Vinci studied anatomy. Da Vinci made many drawings of the human body. The drawings helped people understand the human body.

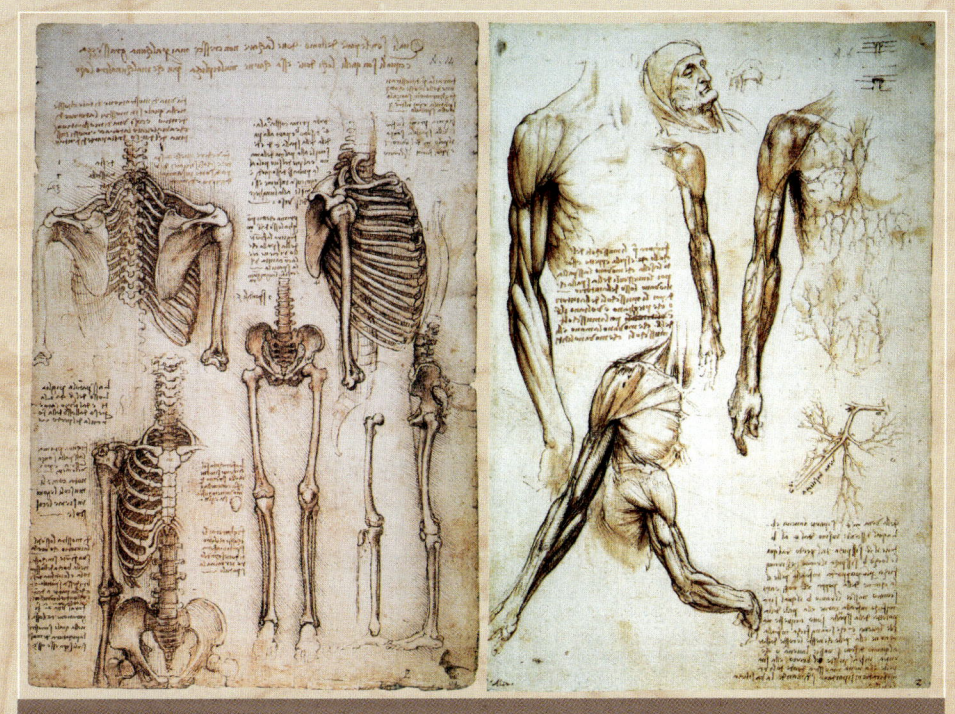

▲ Da Vinci made drawings of the human body.

It's a Fact

Da Vinci used dead people to study the human body. Da Vinci drew the outside of the body. He drew the inside of the body, too.

Chapter 2

Scholars learned many facts about anatomy. Scholars studied how blood moves through the body. Scholars studied how the heart works. Scholars studied how the brain works.

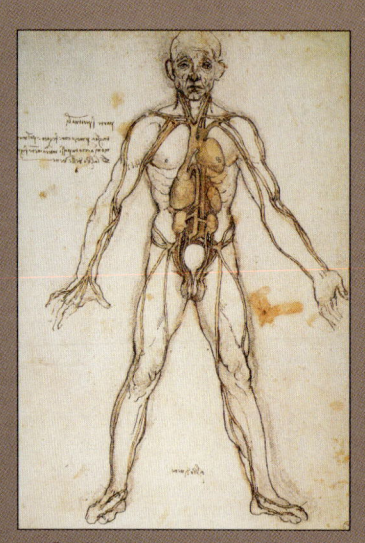

▲ Scholars studied how blood moves.

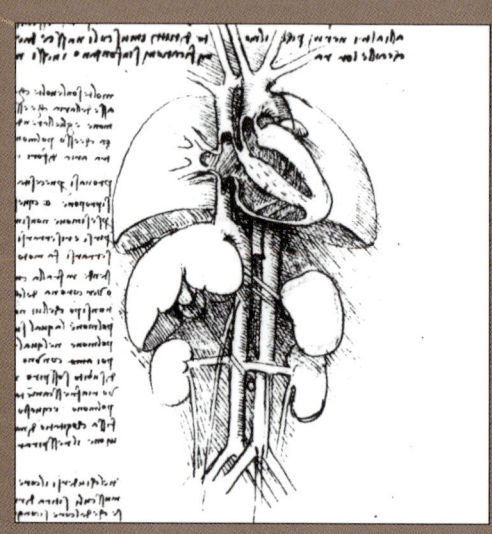

▲ Scholars studied the heart.

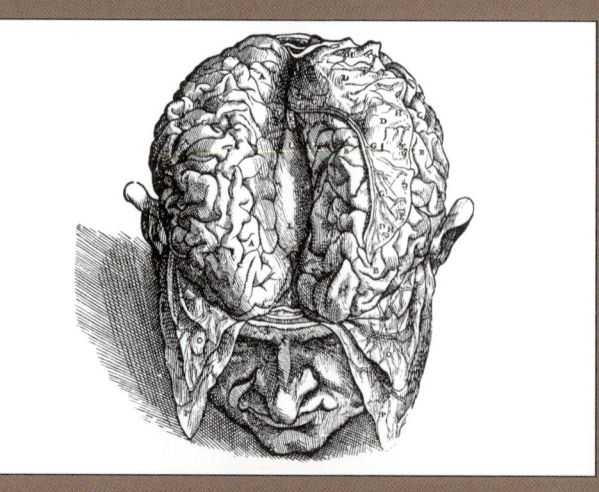

▲ Scholars studied the brain.

What Did People Discover During the Renaissance?

The new facts changed science. The new facts helped doctors. The new facts helped make life better for people.

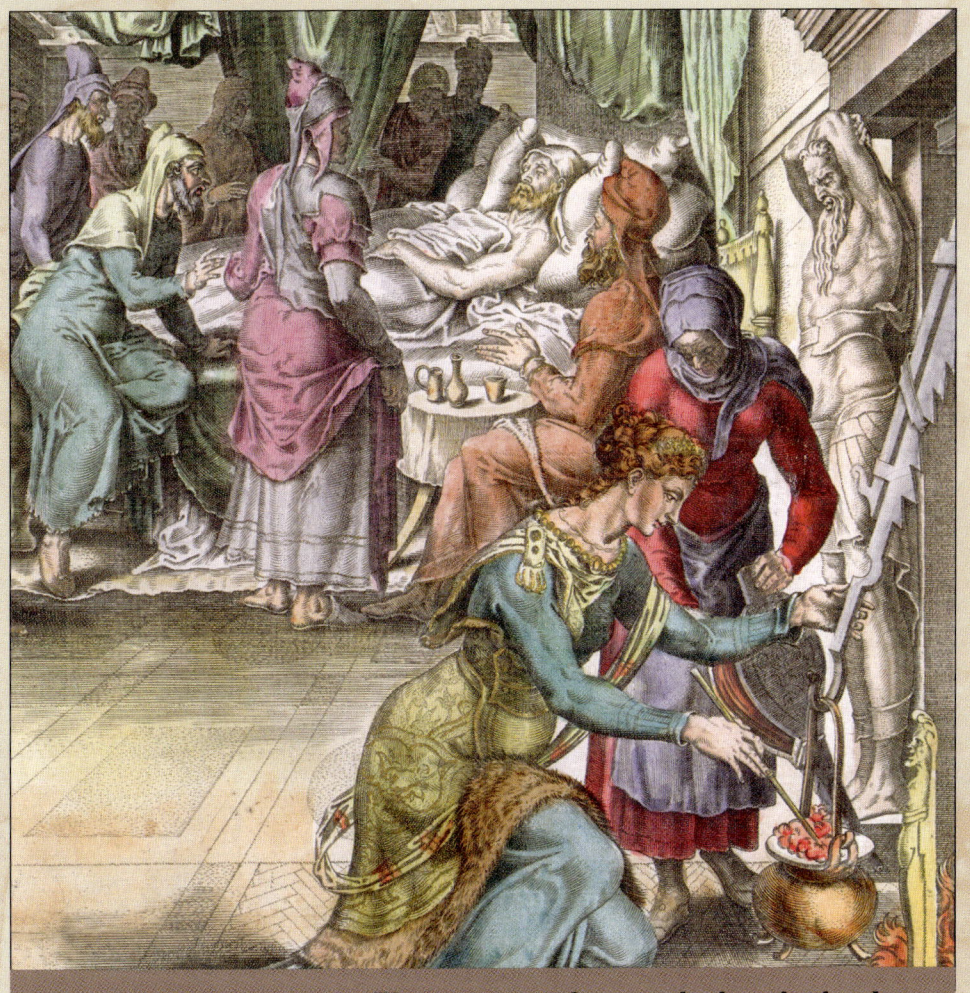

▲ The new science helped doctors.

Chapter 3

What Did People Invent During the Renaissance?

The Renaissance was a time for **inventions**.

Johann Gutenberg invented a printing press in 1448. Johann Gutenberg invented a better printing press. The new printing press had letters that moved. People moved the letters to make different words. The new printing press was faster.

▲ Gutenberg invented a better printing press.

▲ Johann Gutenberg

Did You Know?

Chinese people had printing first. People carved words on wooden blocks. People put ink on the blocks. Then people pressed the wooden blocks on paper.

The new printing press helped people during the Renaissance. People had more books. People learned about new ideas. People learned new facts.

▲ The printing press helped people learn.

Chapter 3

Galileo invented a telescope in 1609. Galileo invented a better telescope. Galileo invented a stronger telescope. His telescope helped scholars learn about the universe.

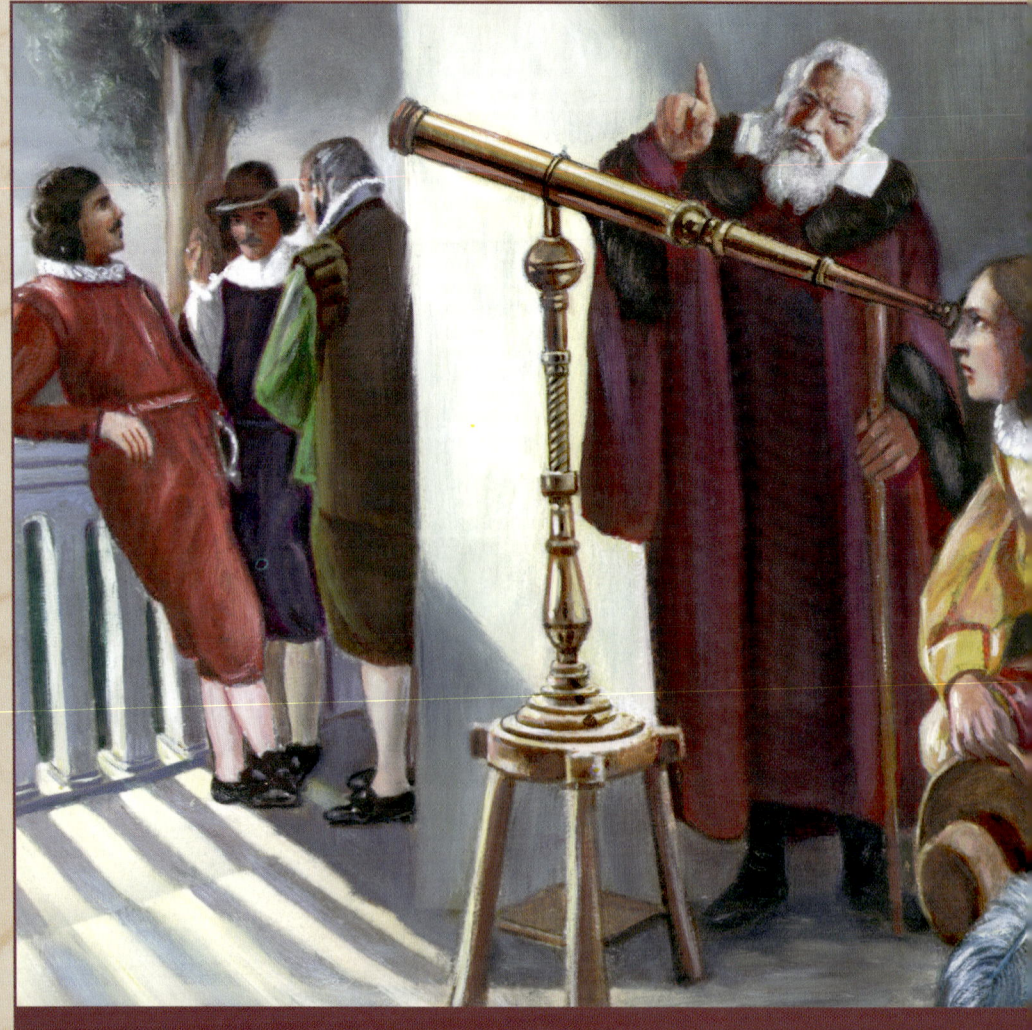

▲ Galileo invented a better telescope.

What Did People Invent During the Renaissance?

Galileo used a telescope to study the planets. Galileo saw the moon. Galileo saw planets. He saw spots on the sun. Stronger telescopes proved new ideas about the universe. Stronger telescopes helped people learn more about science.

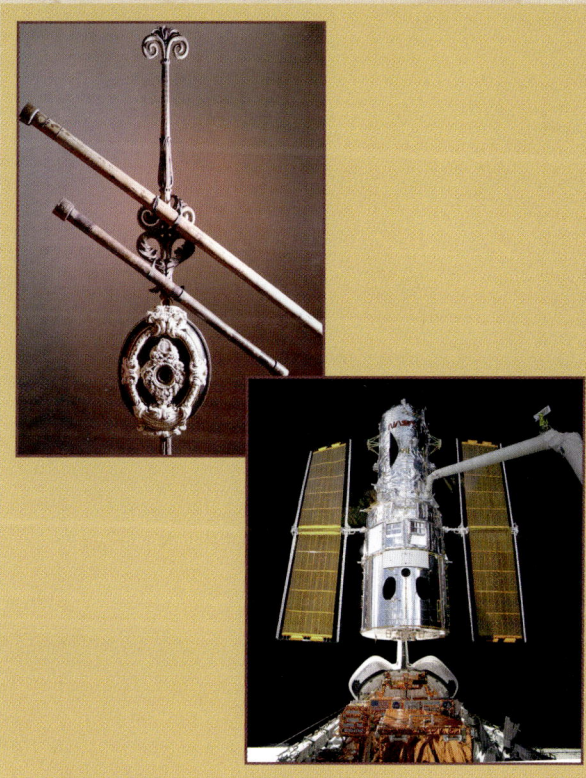

Then and Now

Galileo invented a stronger telescope during the Renaissance. The telescope made planets appear much closer. The Hubble Space Telescope travels around Earth today. The telescope shows planets trillions of miles away.

Chapter 3

People invented a new compass. The new compass was better. The new compass was more accurate. The new compass helped people sail across the oceans. It helped people find new lands.

▲ **People invented a better compass.**

What Did People Invent During the Renaissance?

People invented new ways to make maps. The new maps were better. The new maps were more accurate. The new maps helped sailors. The maps showed the places explorers found.

Make a Connection

Look at the map. How is this map like the maps you know? How do you use maps?

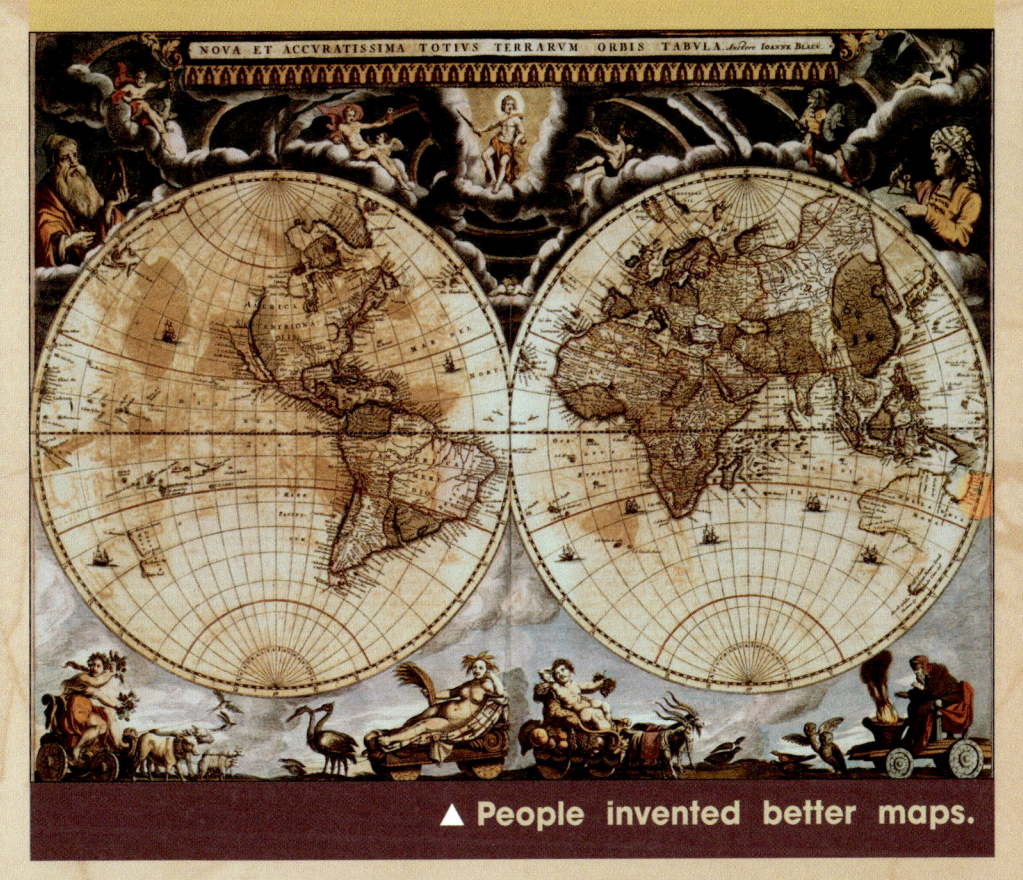

▲ People invented better maps.

Chapter 3

Leonardo da Vinci was a great scholar. Da Vinci had ideas for many inventions. Da Vinci made many drawings of his ideas.

Da Vinci thought about a flying machine. Da Vinci made drawings of flying machines.

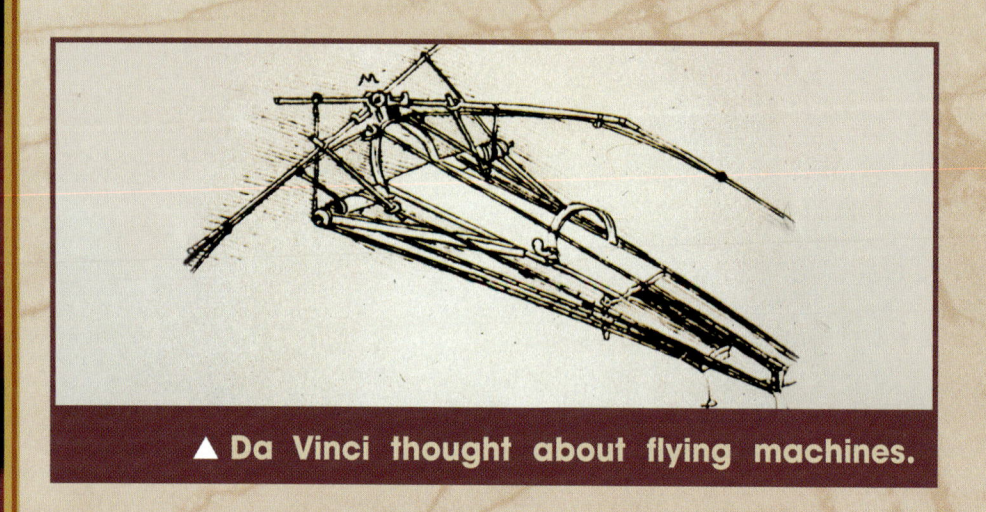

▲ Da Vinci thought about flying machines.

Da Vinci had an idea for a helicopter.

▲ Da Vinci thought about helicopters.

What Did People Invent During the Renaissance?

The parachute was another idea that da Vinci had. Da Vinci had the idea about a parachute first.

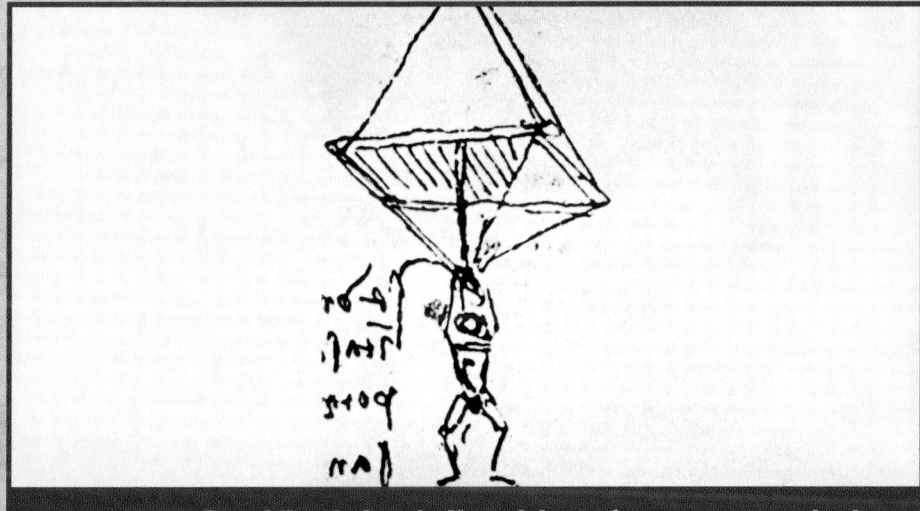

▲ Da Vinci had the idea for a parachute.

Da Vinci never made most of the inventions. People thought the ideas were too strange. People today know da Vinci had great ideas. People today know da Vinci was a great inventor.

Did You Know?

Da Vinci had the idea for the first robot. Da Vinci did not make the robot. Da Vinci wanted the robot to move.

Summary

Science changed during the Renaissance. Scholars had to prove new ideas. Scholars had to look for facts. Scholars discovered important facts. Scholars invented many important things.

Science During the Renaissance

How Did Science Change During the Renaissance?

- Scholars studied in new ways.
- Scholars had to prove new ideas.
- Scholars had to use facts.
- Scholars used observation.
- Scholars began to use math.
- Scholars began to use new tools.
- Science became more accurate.
- People used the scientific method.

What Did People Discover During the Renaissance?

- facts about Earth
- facts about the universe
- facts about anatomy

What Did People Invent During the Renaissance?

- a better printing press
- a better telescope
- a new compass
- new maps

Think About It
1. How did the Renaissance change science?
2. What were the important discoveries?
3. What were the important inventions?

Glossary

accurate true or without mistakes

*The facts had to be **accurate**.*

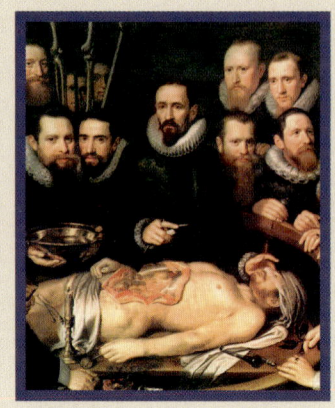

anatomy the study of how the body works

*Scholars discovered facts about **anatomy**.*

astronomer a person who studies the universe

*Nicolaus Copernicus was an **astronomer**.*

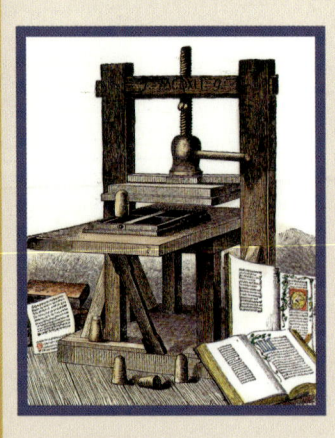

inventions new things made from new ideas

*The Renaissance was a time for **inventions**.*

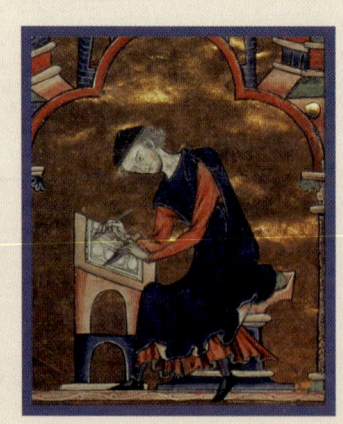

prove to show the truth with facts

*Scholars used facts to **prove** new ideas.*

the Renaissance a time in European history

***The Renaissance** was a time in history.*

scholars people with great knowledge

Scholars studied the world in new ways.

science an area of study

Science changed because of the Renaissance.

scientific method the rules for proving science

*The **scientific method** uses facts to prove ideas.*

universe everything in space

*Scholars studied the **universe** in new ways.*

Index

accurate, 6, 8, 13, 24–25
anatomy, 11, 17–18
artist, 16
astronomer, 12, 14–15
blood, 18
brain, 18
compass, 24
Copernicus, Nicolaus, 12–15
da Vinci, Leonardo, 16–17, 26–27
doctors, 19
drawings, 17, 26
Earth, 10, 12–14
explorers, 25
facts, 6, 8–11, 14, 18–19, 21, 28
Galileo, 14–15, 22–23
Gutenberg, Johann, 20
helicopter, 26
human body, 11, 17–18
inventions, 20, 26–27
Kepler, Johannes, 15
maps, 25
math, 7
paintings, 16
planets, 12–13, 15, 23
printing press, 20–21
prove, 6, 8–9, 14, 23, 28
Renaissance, the, 2–4, 6, 10, 12, 14–16, 20–21, 28
scholars, 5–8, 10–11, 17–18, 22, 26, 28
science, 2–6, 8–9, 19, 23, 28
scientific method, 9
sculptures, 16
sun, 13–15, 23
telescope, 22–23
universe, 5, 10, 12–13, 22–23